Basic Data Structures:

Overview

Aditya Chatterjee x Ue Kiao

BE A NATIONAL PROGRAMMER

In early 1990s, Prof. Paul was excited as his research group was ready to bring an end to a long-standing problem. Excitement ended when they realized the code may take decades to complete execution.

6 years later, when I came, we developed a novel data structure for the problem and reduced execution time to 2 months. It was a major milestone.

INTRODUCTION

Data Structures are one of the most fundamental concepts in Computer Science. It is the study of how we handle data or give a structure to it.

Using the correct data structure in the correct algorithm and problem improves the overall performance significantly.

This book has covered:

- Over 30 data structures
- Images for each data structure to help you visualize the data structures [**IMPORTANT**]
- Basic ideas, advantages, disadvantages, and key thoughts for all data structures.
- Time and space complexity of basic operations for quick reference.

The book is a perfect fit as a starting point to get the complete idea of the entire domain and then, go into each data structure in depth or recreate the details by thinking.

This book is a good fit for you if you:

- Want to get an idea of different Data Structures without going into the details and implementations.

- have solved Algorithmic problems previously and need to revise the complete idea of Basic Data Structures quickly in a day for an upcoming Interview or just for stimulating your brain.

This book has covered over 30 basic data structures starting with Array and up to useful data structures like Trie and Union Find and data structures for specific applications like Graph Algorithms, Dynamic Programming and much more.

As you go through this book, you will form a good understanding of different data structures in contrast and will be able to answer tough research questions with original thought.

We have presented some insightful questions based on these basic Data Structures at the end. Let us get started with the most fundamental data structure in computing systems: Array.

Best of Luck for your Coding Interview.

Book **Basic Data Structures: Overview**

Series: Day before Coding Interview [DCI]

Authors (2): Aditya Chatterjee, Ue Kiao

About the authors:

Aditya Chatterjee is an Independent Researcher, Technical Author and the Founding Member of OPENGENUS, a scientific community focused on Computing Technology.

Ue Kiao is a Japanese Software Developer and has played key role in designing systems like TaoBao, AliPay and many more. She has completed her B. Sc in Mathematics and Computing Science at National Taiwan University and PhD at Tokyo Institute of Technology.

Published: 30 July 2020 (1st Edition)

Current Revision: 08 September 2024 (5th Edition)

Pages: 71

Publisher: OpenGenus

Contact: team@opengenus.org

Available on Amazon as E-book, Paperback and Hardcover exclusively.

TABLE OF CONTENTS

RECOMMENDED BOOKS

DAILY43: Best way to master EASY tagged Coding problems in a month with to-the-point explanation.

No need to practice 1000s of problems over years. This book covers all coding patterns.

Get **DAILY43** on Amazon: **amzn.to/4cVoEdK**

Series you should read:

- Day before Coding Interview [DCI] series: **amzn.to/3XAH8f9**
- Coding Interview DSA series: **amzn.to/3z7NbOQ**

Array

Array is a linear data structure for storing data elements sequentially (one after another) in physical memory. Physical Memory have memory cells line up one by one internally and array takes up a group of contiguous cells.

This is the most fundamental data structure in our Computer Architecture. It has its root from the early theoretical models of Computers like Turing Machine. This is from a time when there was no real Computer.

Denoted as array[].

i^{th} element is denoted as array[i].

Index or position starts from 0. **Visualize as follows**:

5	11	7	-9	100	99

Index 0 1 2 3 4 5

If there are N data elements of size D bytes, then **N x D bytes will be allocated**, and we need to keep only the starting address to ensure access to it.

Basic operations:

- Insertion: takes O(1) time
- Deletion: takes O(1) time
- Traversal: takes O(N) time
- Accessing N^{th} element: O(1) time

Following table summarizes the performance:

Attribute	Array		
	Average case	Worst Case	Best Case
Insertion	O(1)	O(1)	O(1)
Deletion	O(1)	O(1)	O(1)
Access	O(1)	O(1)	O(1)
Traversal	O(N)	O(N)	O(N)
Memory	O(N)	O(N)	O(N)

Advantages:

- Insertion and deletion takes place in constant time O(1)
- Accessing a random element by index is faster as we can calculate the address directly
- Does not store any extra information

Disadvantages:

- Difficult (not possible in general) to increase overall size once defined as we need sequential memory which may not be available
- For large data, array is not preferred due to above point as memory allocation may fail.

Key thoughts:

- Arrays are fundamentally supported in all major programming languages
- It is the simplest way of handling data
- This may change if we change our fundamental computer architecture
- Access takes constant time $O(1)$ as we have the destination address but the computing system may go through memory locations linearly.

Dynamic Array

Dynamic Array is a modification to the classical Array which overcomes the limitation of resizing the array while maintaining the key advantages of an array that is constant time insertion and deletion.

Original array:

5	11	7	-9	100	99

Index 0   1   2   3   4   5

Can decrease in size:

5	11	7	-9	100

Index 0   1   2   3   4

Can increase in size:

5	11	7	-9	100	99	19

Index 0   1   2   3   4   5   6

Basic operations:

- Insertion: takes $O(1)$ time on average; $O(N)$ worst case on resizing

- Deletion: takes O(1) time on average; O(N) worst case on resizing
- Traversal: takes O(1) time
- Accessing N^{th} element: O(1) time
- Resizing: takes O(N) time to copy all elements

Following table summarizes the performance:

Attribute	Dynamic Array		
	Average case	Worst Case	Best Case
Insertion	O(1)	O(N)	O(1)
Deletion	O(1)	O(N)	O(1)
Access	O(1)	O(1)	O(1)
Traversal	O(N)	O(N)	O(N)
Memory	O(N)	O(N)	O(N)
Resizing	O(1)	O(N)	O(N)

Advantages:

- Overcomes the disadvantage of fixed size of arrays
- Maintains the constant time performance of insertion and deletion operation on average
- Does not store any extra information

Disadvantages:

- Insertion and deletion operation take linear time O(N) in the worst case (but the occurrence decreases exponentially)

- Does not utilize the system memory well (same as array) as it requires sequential memory

Key thoughts:

- This brings in a good point that we need to consider average performance that is *"performance over several operations"*.
- There are other variants/ improvements to this version or array in general. The basic performance remains same but requires deep insights to understand it.
- As for the naming, *"dynamic"* comes from the fact that the size of the array is changing based on the operations.

Following table summarizes the difference between Array and Dynamic Array clearly:

Attribute	Array		Dynamic Array	
	Average case	Worst Case	Average case	Worst Case
Insertion	O(1)	O(1)	O(1)	O(N)
Deletion	O(1)	O(1)	O(1)	O(N)
Access	O(1)	O(1)	O(1)	O(N)
Traversal	O(N)	O(N)	O(N)	O(N)
Memory	O(N)	O(N)	O(N)	O(N)

Singly Linked List

Linked List is the generalization of array where we store the address of the next element along with the data of the current element. We keep track of the address of the first element only.

In singly Linked List, each element keeps track of its own data and the address of the next element only.

If there are N data elements of size D bytes and address size is M bytes, then **N x (D + M - 1) bytes will be allocated**, and we need to keep only the starting address to ensure access to it. The (-1) is because the next node of last node will be NULL.

Basic operations:

- Insertion: takes O(N) time
- Deletion: takes O(N) time
- Traversal: takes O(N) time
- Accessing Nth element: O(N) time
- Get previous element: O(N) time
- Get next element: O(1) time

Visualize a Singly Linked List as:

Advantages:

- Utilizes system memory well (compared to array). It will work till there is memory available in the computing system.

Disadvantages:

- Stores additional data that is the address for each data element which is not memory efficient.
- Insertion and deletion operation take linear time O(N)
- Finding the previous element takes linear time O(N) as we have to begin traversal from the starting/ head node again.

Following table summarizes the differences between Array and Singly Linked List:

Attribute	Array		Singly Linked List	
	Average case	Worst Case	Average case	Worst Case
Insertion	O(1)	O(1)	O(N)	O(N)
Deletion	O(1)	O(1)	O(N)	O(N)
Access	O(1)	O(1)	O(N)	O(N)
Traversal	O(N)	O(N)	O(N)	O(N)
Previous	O(1)	O(1)	O(N)	O(N)
Next	O(1)	O(1)	O(1)	O(1)
Memory	N	N	N*(D+M-1)	N*(D+M-1)

Note: Linked List are more reliable than array when memory of the system is fragmented (has small fragments of free memory).

Doubly Linked List

In Doubly Linked List, we store the memory address of the previous element in addition to the data we store in Singly Linked List.

If there are N data elements of size D bytes and address size is M bytes, then **N x (D + 2 x M - 2) bytes will be allocated**, and we need to keep only the starting address to ensure access to it. This is more than Singly Linked List. The (-2) is because the previous node of head node and the next node of last node will be NULL.

Visualize a Doubly Linked List as:

Basic operations:

- Insertion: takes O(N) time
- Deletion: takes O(N) time
- Traversal: takes O(N) time
- Accessing Nth element: O(N) time
- Get previous element: O(1) time
- Get next element: O(1) time

Notice the improvement in case of getting the previous element.

Advantages:

- We can get the previous element in constant time $O(1)$ which takes linear time $O(N)$ for Singly Linked List
- We can traverse either directions from a given point
- It is more flexible and proves to be more efficient for specific algorithms

Disadvantages:

- It requires more memory (compared to Singly Linked List) which can be an issue for memory constrained systems.

Key thoughts:

- This brings up a good point that a simple modification in the data structure can improve the performance of a specific operation.
- In this case, storing more information results in doing a specific operation in constant time $O(1)$. This may seems obvious but it is not this simple.

Circular Linked List

Circular Linked List is a modification of a Linked List where the last element stores the address of the first element as the next element (instead of null). This property can be applied to both Singly Linked List and Doubly Linked List which results in two types:

- Circular Singly Linked List
- Circular Doubly Linked List

In terms of memory, it requires to store only one additional memory address.

Visualize a Circular Linked List as:

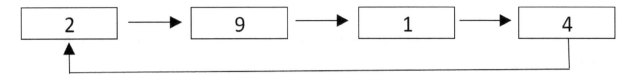

Basic operations:

- Insertion: takes O(N) time
- Deletion: takes O(N) time
- Traversal: takes O(N) time
- Accessing Nth element: O(N) time
- Get previous element: O(1) time (for Doubly Linked List) and O(N) time (for Singly Linked List)

- Get next element: O(1) time

Advantages:

- We need not handle NULL as a special case. This might look simple but has been the cause of major bugs in real systems.
- Any element can be considered as first or last element and hence, it is flexible.

Disadvantages:

- Code must ensure that it does not get trapped in a loop.

Key thoughts:

- While designing a data structure, one must consider eliminating special cases to avoid software bugs.

Following table summarizes the difference between the variants of Linked List clearly:

Attribute	Singly Linked List	Doubly Linked List	Circular Singly LL	Circular Doubly LL
Insertion	O(N)	O(N)	O(N)	O(N)
Deletion	O(N)	O(N)	O(N)	O(N)
Access	O(N)	O(N)	O(N)	O(N)
Traversal	O(N)	O(N)	O(N)	O(N)
Previous	O(N)	O(1)	O(N)	O(1)
Next	O(1)	O(1)	O(1)	O(1)

Memory	N*(D+M-1)	N*(D+2M-2)	N*(D+M)	N*(D+2M)

We will now, move to a modification of Linked List which brings in new ideas to model problems.

Stack

Stack is a data structure which maintains an order among the elements based on the order the elements have been added. The top element is the element that has been inserted last. It is known as "**Last in First Out**".

It can be implemented with Array or Linked List.

Visualize a Stack as:

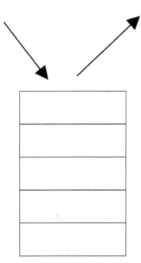

Operations:

- Push (Insert): O(1) in Array, O(1) in Linked List
- Pop (Delete): O(1) in Array, O(1) in Linked List
- Peek (Check element at top): O(1) in Array, O(1) in Linked List

Note: Time complexity depends on the implementation and we assume the best possible implementation.

| Attribute | Stack | | | |
| | Array | | Linked List | |
	Average	Worst	Average	Worst
Push	O(1)	O(1)	O(1)	O(1)
Pop	O(1)	O(1)	O(1)	O(1)
Peek	O(1)	O(1)	O(1)	O(1)
Memory	(N+1)*D	(N+1)*D	N*(D+M-1)	N*(D+M-1)

Advantages:

- Maintains order among elements without any overhead
- Useful in several algorithms

Disadvantages:

- No drawback from the point of the features it supports

Key Thoughts:

- It is a modification of basic data structures like array and linked list and adds one additional rule
- Changing these rules or adding more rules give rise to other data structures

Queue

Queue is in the same line as Stack with the exception that the first element inserted and the first element in the list. It is known as *"First In First Out"*.

Visualize a Queue as:

Operations:

- Push/ Enqueue: O(1) on average
- Pop/ Dequeue: O(1) on average
- Peek: O(1) on average

Following table summarizes the performance:

Attribute	Queue			
	Array		Linked List	
	Average	Worst	Average	Worst
Push	O(1)	O(1)	O(1)	O(1)
Pop	O(1)	O(1)	O(1)	O(1)
Peek	O(1)	O(1)	O(1)	O(1)
Memory	(N+1)*D	(N+1)*D	N*(D+M)	N*(D+M)

Note: We need to store the top and end position of Queue to make the operations optimal.

Advantages:

- Maintains order among elements without any overhead
- Useful in several algorithms

Disadvantages:

- We need to store top and end position to implement it optimally (*Compare this with Stack*)

Key thoughts:

- This is opposite of Stack Data Structure

- Maintaining Stack optimally requires us to store less information than in case of Queue

Deque (Double ended Queue)

Deque is a modification of Queue where we add additional operations to support addition and removal of elements from both sides.

$$Deque = Queue + Stack$$

Visualize a Deque as:

Basic Operations:

- Push Front: O(1) time on average
- Push Back: O(1) time on average
- Pop Front: O(1) time on average
- Pop Back: O(1) time on average
- Peek Front: O(1) time on average
- Peek Back: O(1) time on average

Following table summarizes the performance:

Attribute	Double Ended Queue			
	Array		Linked List	
	Average	Worst	Average	Worst
Push Front	O(1)	O(1)	O(1)	O(1)
Push Back	O(1)	O(1)	O(1)	O(1)
Pop Front	O(1)	O(1)	O(1)	O(1)
Pop Back	O(1)	O(1)	O(1)	O(1)
Peek Front	O(1)	O(1)	O(1)	O(1)
Peek Back	O(1)	O(1)	O(1)	O(1)
Memory	(N+1)*D	(N+1)*D	N*(D+M)	N*(D+M)

Advantages:

- Deque can be used as a queue or stack alternatively
- It acts like a generalized data structure and allows switching without any overhead.

Disadvantages:

- If not used correctly, a deque intended to be used as a queue and be misused as a stack.

Key thoughts:

- Implementing deque efficiently requires experience. Think and try it.
- This brings up a good point that adding new features does not necessarily slow down a data structure

Circular Queue

Circular Queue is a queue which has no end. More precisely, it is an implementation strategy that uses a Circular Linked List or replicate it in an array.

The top and bottom index of a circular queue is flexible. In previous variants of queue, top index may be fixed to 0.

Visualize a circular queue as follows:

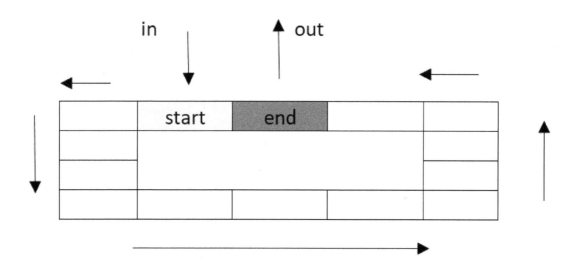

Basic operations:

- Push/ Enqueue: O(1) on average
- Pop/ Dequeue: O(1) on average
- Peek: O(1) on average

Following table summarizes the performance:

Attribute	Circular Queue			
	Array		Linked List	
	Average	Worst	Average	Worst
Push	O(1)	O(1)	O(1)	O(1)
Pop	O(1)	O(1)	O(1)	O(1)
Peek	O(1)	O(1)	O(1)	O(1)
Memory	(N+1)*D	(N+1)*D	N*(D+M)	N*(D+M)

Advantages:

- Makes the implementation flexible
- Utilizes the available space in case of array better

Disadvantages:

- It can result in confusion/ bug in code if extra features like traversal are not handled correctly

Key thoughts:

- It illustrates the idea that the same thing can be implemented in different ways
- Same internal attributes of a data structure like top and bottom indexes can be handled differently.

Binary Tree

Binary Tree is a data structure like Doubly Linked List but is looked upon differently. Each element stores three information:

- Its own data
- Memory address of another element (known as left child)
- Memory address of another element (known as right child)

Visualize a Binary Tree as follows:

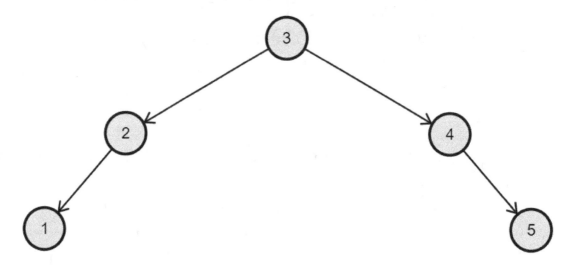

The right child of node/ element 2 is NULL while both child of node 1 is NULL.

There are two variants:

- Balanced Binary Tree
- Unbalanced Binary Tree

A Binary Tree is balanced if the difference in height of the left sub-tree and right sub-tree for every node is at most 1. This results in the height of the binary search tree to be **log N** (minimum) where there are N elements in the tree.

If the Binary Tree is not balanced, then it is Unbalanced Binary Tree. In this case, the height of the binary Tree is larger than log N with the worst case as N (same as Singly Linked List).

This is how an extreme Unbalanced Binary Tree looks like:

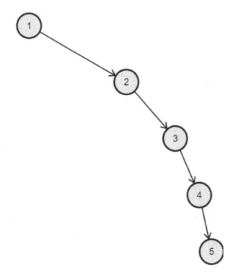

In terms of memory, if there are N data elements of size D bytes and address size is M bytes, then **N * (D+2M)** bytes of memory is allocated. This assumes that we assign memory for address of NULL elements as well.

If we consider NULL, we shall consider two extreme cases:

- Balanced Binary Tree: **(N/2) * (D+2M) + N/2 bytes**
- Extreme Unbalanced Binary Tree: **(N-1) * (D+M) + D bytes**

Basic Operations:

- Insertion: O(log N) time on average, O(N) worst case
- Deletion: O(log N) time on average, O(N) worst case
- Traversal: O(N) time

Following table summarizes the performance:

Attribute	Binary Tree		
	Average case	**Worst Case**	**Best Case**
Insertion	O(log N)	O(N)	O(log N)
Deletion	O(log N)	O(N)	O(log N)
Traversal	O(N)	O(N)	O(N)
Memory	(N-1) * (D+M)	(N-1) * (D+M) + D	(N/2) * (D+2M) + N/2

Advantages:

- Binary Tree relies on the idea of dividing a dataset repeatedly into two smaller parts. This is useful when data follow a relative relation.
- When Balanced, it is useful for various applications/ algorithms.

Disadvantages:

- When unbalanced, it resembles a Singly Linked List but may significantly degrade performance when used like a Binary Tree

Key thoughts:

- This brings a new structure to the data
- The idea is to eliminate multiple elements by analyzing one element

Binary Search Tree

Binary Search Tree is an improvement over Binary Tree where the focus to order elements based on relative order. The left child element must be smaller than the current element and the right child element must be greater than the current element.

The best performance is achieved on Balanced Binary Search Tree where search operation takes $O(\log N)$ time instead of $O(N)$ time as with our previous data structures.

Operations:

- Insertion: takes $O(\log N)$ on average
- Deletion: takes $O(\log N)$ on average
- Searching: takes $O(\log N)$ on average

Following is the summary of the operations:

Attribute	Binary Search Tree		
	Average case	Worst Case	Best Case
Insertion	$O(\log N)$	$O(N)$	$O(\log N)$
Deletion	$O(\log N)$	$O(N)$	$O(\log N)$
Searching	$O(\log N)$	$O(N)$	$O(1)$
Memory	(N-1) * (D+M)	(N-1) * (D+M) + D	(N/2) * (D+2M) + N/2

Advantages:

- Searching is exponentially faster than in traditional data structures like Array and Linked List
- Binary Search Tree, potentially, reduces the search space of size O(N) to O(log N) which is a significant improvement.

Disadvantages:

- It works well only when it is balanced or else it performs like a general Binary Tree.

Key thoughts:

- This is an important data structure as it divides the search into smaller search spaces. This leads to *"Space Partitioning Data Structures"*

AVL Tree

As we learnt from the last few data structures, Binary Tree is useful only when it is balanced. To overcome this, there are several self-balancing Binary Trees which can maintain their height to O(log N) by adding a balancing operation along with insertion and deletion operation.

AVL Tree is one of the simplest self-balancing Binary Tree.

The basic idea is to add a new property: *"The difference of height of left and right sub-tree must be at most 1"*. Insertion and deletion operations are following by a balancing operation to maintain this property.

Visualize an AVL Tree as follows:

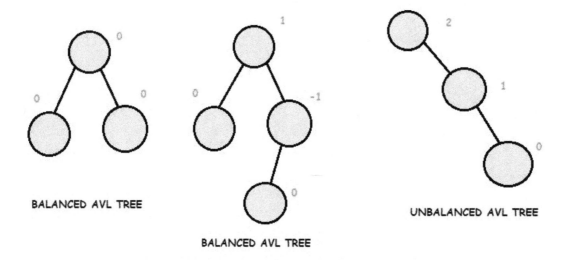

BALANCED AVL TREE

BALANCED AVL TREE

UNBALANCED AVL TREE

The values 0,1,-1,2 are balance factor of the nodes.

BalanceFactor = height of right subtree – height of left subtree

To keep itself balanced, an AVL tree may perform four kinds of rotations:

- Left rotation (LL Rotation)
- Right rotation (RR Rotation)
- Left-Right rotation (LR Rotation)
- Right-Left rotation (RL Rotation)

Left Rotation

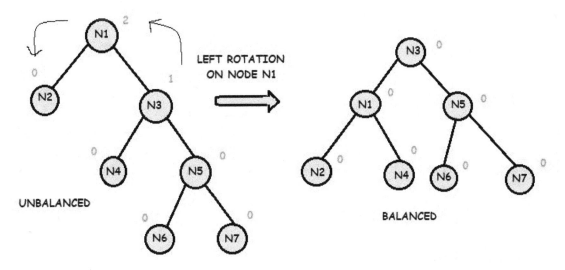

Right Rotation

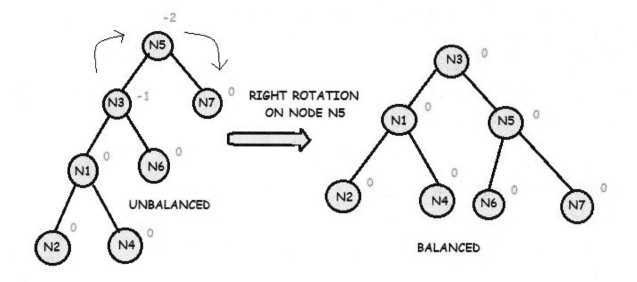

Left Right Rotation

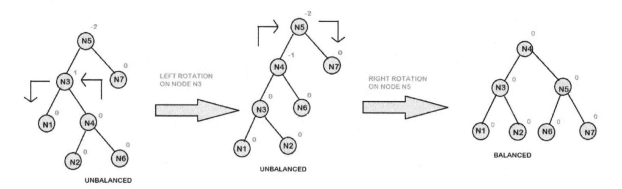

Right Left Rotation

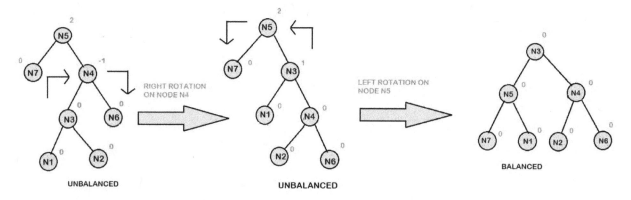

Operations:

- Insertion: takes O(log N) on average
- Deletion: takes O(log N) on average
- Searching: takes O(log N) on average
- Traversal: takes O(N) on average

This table summarizes the performance:

Attribute	AVL Tree		
	Average case	Worst Case	Best Case
Insertion	O(log N)	O(log N)	O(log N)
Deletion	O(log N)	O(log N)	O(log N)
Searching	O(log N)	O(log N)	O(1)
Memory	Same as best case	Same as best case	(N/2) * (D+2M) + N/2

Notice the improvement in worst case performance.

Advantages:

- Tree always stays balanced

Disadvantages:

- There are no specific disadvantages considering it is a Binary Tree

Key thoughts:

- Adding a simple restructuring operation enables a data structure to maintain the best shape without any overall overhead

Hash Map

Searching initially took linear time O(N) with data structures like array, linked list and binary tree. This improved to O(log N) with Balanced Binary Search time.

With Hash Map, we take this to the next level by searching in constant time O(1).

The idea of Hash Map is to use an array to store the elements and determine the index for a given element using a hash function.

The challenge is if the hash function maps two different elements to the same index. The solution involves using a linked list for each array element and other approaches. These are known as *"collision resolution"*.

Hash Map is basically an array where the index is the element and the actual element denotes if the index is a valid element (1) or not (0).

Visualize it as:

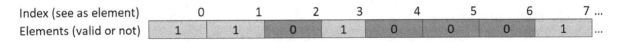

Index (see as element)	0	1	2	3	4	5	6	7 ...
Elements (valid or not)	1	1	0	1	0	0	0	1 ...

Operations:

- Insertion: O(1) average case
- Deletion: O(1) average case
- Searching: O(1) average case

The summary of the performance of the operations is as follows:

Attribute	Hash Map		
	Average case	Worst Case	Best Case
Insertion	O(1)	O(N)	O(1)
Deletion	O(1)	O(N)	O(1)
Searching	O(1)	O(N)	O(1)
Memory	N	N	N

Advantages:

- Searching takes place in constant time which is a significant improvement
- Does not store any extra information like in Binary Tree, Linked List and others; This is because it uses Array as the underlying data structure.

Disadvantages:

- Space requirements are usually high but there are workarounds which can make average/ real time performance comparable to other data structures.

Multi-dimensional Array

Multi-dimensional Array is an array which provides multiple indexes to specify. It is, usually, used to divide data into different categories.

For example: An image is seen as a 2D data with height and width. The array for this is defined as:

Array data[height][width]

In memory, it is stored as a 1-dimensional array. There are two approaches for this:

- Row major
- Column major

In Row major, each row is stored sequentially in memory as a 1D array.

Example: [row 1 elements], [row 2 elements], …

In Column major, each column is stored sequentially in memory as a 1D array. Example: [column 1 elements], [column 2 elements], …

For a 2D array with dimensions HxW and index (i, j) stored row major, the actual index is **i*W + j**. If it would have been stored column major, the actual index would have been **j*H + i**.

Basic operations:

- Insertion: takes O(1) time
- Deletion: takes O(1) time
- Traversal: takes O(N) time
- Accessing Nth element: O(1) time

Following table summarizes the performance:

Attribute	Array		
	Average case	**Worst Case**	**Best Case**
Insertion	O(1)	O(1)	O(1)
Deletion	O(1)	O(1)	O(1)
Access	O(1)	O(1)	O(1)
Traversal	O(N)	O(N)	O(N)
Memory	O(N)	O(N)	O(N)

Advantages:

- Gives a structure to the data in a simple way without use of OOP concepts
- Useful in closely representing matrix operations

Disadvantages:

- Access seems to be constant time, but reality is we get the address in constant time but reaching the location is sequential (hence, takes linear time).
- Need to consider row major/ column major to efficiently implement an algorithm

Key thoughts:

- This brings the idea that even complex data structures are just data points like an array in memory.

User defined data structures

User defined data structures are custom implementations of data structures which are not already supported by the programming language directly.

For example: Array is a built-in data structure in most programming language like C but AVL Tree (which we explored) is needs to be used as a user defined data structure as:

- AVL Tree is a custom data structure and a language has in-built support of a limited number of data structures that are in the vision of the original developers

Basic operations:

- Depends on the data structure being implemented
- Depends on the specific application and focus (performance, validation, proof of concept or something else)

Advantages:

- Creating a user defined data structure gives us the flexibility to design it according to our needs

- In-built data structures cannot be changed and often, come with extra features that are an overhead for high performance applications

Disadvantages:

- The only disadvantage is that implementing a data structure from scratch takes time, but the advantages are great.

Key thoughts:

- This is more of an implementation point of view of Data Structures

Array of user defined structures

Array of user defined data structure is an array where elements are user defined data structures.

A simple 1-dimensional array has an in-built data structure like integer as an element.

A multi-dimensional array may be an array where an array element is an array itself. The recursive depth of this continues till the point as allowed by the dimension of the Multi-dimensional array.

Some examples:

- Array of Linked Lists
- Array of Binary Tree
- Array of AVL Tree
- Array of Hash Map

The first two (Array of Linked Lists and Array of Binary Tree) are used as collision handling techniques in Hash Map.

Basic operations:

- Access specific index: O(1) on average

- Traversal: O(1) on average + Time complexity of the user defined data structure

Advantages:

- Enable us to use array along with custom data structures

Disadvantages:

- There are no specific disadvantages considering the purpose of this structure

Key thoughts:

- Using the programming language at hand effectively is the key to designing efficient Data Structures
- Every language has a different set of strategies and it is important to be aware of the tools available.

Graph Data Structures

There are 2 basic data structures that are used to represent a Graph problem. These are:

- Adjacency Matrix
- Adjacency List

Adjacency Matrix

Adjacency Matrix is a 2-dimensional (2D) array that is used to represent a graph where both rows and columns denote vertices and the values denote edges between the concerned vertices (indexes).

Adjacency Matrix = 2D array

Visualize it as:

Vertex	1	2	3	4
1	0	1	1	0
2	1	0	0	0
3	1	0	0	1
4	0	0	1	0

(0 denotes edge is not present)

(1 denotes edge is present between the two nodes)

Basic operations:

- Verify edge between vertices: O(1) on average
- Find vertices that linked to a vertex: O(N) time for K connected vertices
- Traversal in a graph of V nodes and E edges: $O(V^2)$
- Memory for a graph with V nodes and E edges: $O(V^2)$

Following table summarizes the performance:

Attribute	Adjacency Matrix		
	Average case	Worst Case	Best Case
Edge between 2 nodes	O(1)	O(1)	O(1)
Traversal	$O(V^2)$	$O(V^2)$	$O(V^2)$
Linked vertices	O(V)	O(V)	O(V)
Memory	$O(V^2)$	$O(V^2)$	$O(V^2)$

Advantages:

- Highly useful for specific problems (like finding paths with K edges) where matrix multiplication can be used.
- Better memory utilization for dense graphs
- Constant time access to verify edge between vertices

Disadvantages:

- Takes linear time O(N) to get the list of vertices linked to a vertex
- For sparse graph, memory is still allocated.

Key thoughts:

- An insightful approach to represent a graph as an array
- This is the basic approach to represent graphical structures. Trees like Binary Search Tree are a specific variant of this even though it may look different.
- Usually, matrix value of 0 means no edge and 1 means an edge exist. In general, other values can be assigned to denote **edge weights**.

Adjacency List

Adjacency List is another graph representation where an array of Linked List is used with each array index representing a vertex (say V) and each Linked List is a list of vertices directly connected to the specific vertex (V).

Adjacency List = Array of Linked List

Visualize it as:

Vertex	Linked List		
1	3	→	4
2	1		
3	1	→	4
4	3		

(array)

Basic operations:

- Verify edge between vertices: O(V) on average
- Find vertices that linked to a vertex: O(K) time for K connected vertices

- Traversal in a graph of V nodes and E edges: O(E)
- Memory for a graph with V nodes and E edges: O(E)

Following table summarizes the idea well:

Attribute	Adjacency List		
	Average case	Worst Case	Best Case
Edge between 2 nodes	O(V)	O(V)	O(1)
Traversal	O(E)	O(E)	O(E)
Linked vertices	O(V)	O(V)	O(V)
Memory	O(E)	O(E)	O(E)

Advantages:

- Memory efficient as it shows data only for connections that exist unlike adjacency matrix that stores default value for all possible connections
- Improves performance of algorithms that rely on going from one node to another node.

Disadvantages:

- The only major drawback is that we cannot verify if an edge exist between two nodes in constant time.
- For dense graph, performance may go down along with memory overhead of maintaining a Linked List.

Key thoughts:

- This brings up a good example where linked list improve the performance greatly.
- Adjacency Matrix can be seen as a worst-case scenario for generalization of Adjacency List
- In real system, sparse graphs are more frequently encountered where Adjacency List performs well for specific approaches.
- Understanding when to choose between Adjacency Matrix and List is a must have skill.
- Think: Can be used: *A Linked List of Linked Lists*

Key thoughts on Graph Data Structures:

- Graph problems can be seen as a representation of search space
- There are advanced data structures to handle search space but these two basic graph data structures are good starting point. *Think of representing 2D map.*

Disjoint Set Data Structure

Disjoint Set Data Structures are data structures that deal with a collection of elements known as sets. It supports that common set operations like union, check which set and more.

Union Find data structure is the most common type and efficient for most applications.

The basic idea of Union Find is that each element will point to the element that is the leader of the given set (or represents the set). In general, an element can link to any element in the set but the ultimate element (on following links) should be the leader element.

Based on this basic idea, operations are performed, and some insightful optimizations are applied to arrive at the most optimized performance.

Basic operations:

- Make Set: O(1) on average
- Find Set: O(a(N)) on average
- Union of two set: O(a(N)) on average

Note: a(N) denotes Inverse Ackermann Function and can be considered as a constant. The maximum value can be 5 for values of N that can be handled by computing devices today.

$$A(N) \sim O(1)$$

Following table summarizes the idea well:

Attribute	Union Find		
	Average case	Worst Case	Best Case
Make Set	O(1)	O(1)	O(1)
Union	O(a(1))	O(N)	O(1)
Find	O(a(1))	O(N)	O(1)
Memory	O(N)	O(N)	O(N)

Advantages:

• Near constant time performance for all operations where using common approach may take linear time.

Disadvantages:

• No specific disadvantage from the point of operations it has been designed for.

Key thoughts:

• The uniqueness of this data structure lies in the complexity analysis.

- It is an example of a data structure that has near perfect performance for all realistic data size.

Data Structure for Strings

Strings are usually represented as an array of characters but most Programming Languages handle string as a separate built-in data structure.

With this, we may need some special data structure to work on string based problems or use previous data structures. There are two key approaches:

- Convert string to integer and use traditional approaches
- Use special data structure

For example: Hash Maps are, frequently, used in string problems like finding sub strings and much more. To get the complete picture of how to solve String based problems, go through this book:

STRING ALGORITHMS FOR THE DAY BEFORE YOUR CODING INTERVIEW

daybefore4.opengenus.org

MUST READ TO GET INTO THE MINDSET OF SOLVING STRING PROBLEMS

Get it now: <u>daybefore4.opengenus.org</u>

One special data structure for strings is **Trie**.

Trie

Trie is a data structure which is used to store strings so that searching and other operations are optimized.

It is similar to tree data structures and the idea is each node will have all characters possible. Each character will point to another node if the character is present in any of the strings. Each node will denote if it is an end of a word.

Basic operations:

- Find: O(C) on average
- Insert: O(C) on average
- Delete: O(C) on average
- Traverse: O(NxC) in the worst case

Where C is number of characters in String and N is number of strings

Following table summarizes the performance of basic operations:

Attribute	Trie		
	Average case	**Worst Case**	**Best Case**
Find	O(C)	O(C)	O(C)
Insert	O(C)	O(C)	O(C)

Delete	O(C)	O(N*C)	O(C)
Traverse	O(N*C)	O(N*C)	O(N*C)
Memory	O(L*N)	O(L*N)	O(L*N)

Note: L is the number of unique character in the language.

Advantages:

- Efficient for specific tasks such as finding similar strings which is difficult in other alternatives (Read the linked book to get the idea completely)
- Does not require string to be converted to numeric data

Disadvantages:

- There are other alternatives but trie is enough for most basic applications.
- Basic operations like searching is slower when string is converted to numeric data.

Key thoughts:

- Trie brings in the idea that smaller problems can be considered as units of a data structure.

Data Structures for Dynamic Programming

Dynamic Programming problems, usually, work well with multi-dimensional arrays where each dimension denotes an attribute of the problem at hand.

This brings a key fundamental idea.

Go through this book to get the idea:

Dynamic Programming for the day before your Coding Interview

daybefore3.opengenus.org

Get it now: daybefore3.opengenus.org

One example:

For the problem of finding the longest palindromic subsequence, one structure we can consider is:

```
dp[j] = length of Longest common increasing subsequence
```

For this, the relations to compute values are:

```
# if a common element is found in both arrays
if arr1[i] == arr2[j]:
    dp[j] = max(current+1, dp[j])

# if arr1 element is greater, current variable is updated
if arr1[i] > arr2[j]:
    current = max(current, dp[j])
```

In this case, we used a 1-dimensional array to represent the problem.

Consider the problem of finding the number of subsets with a given OR value. One structure we can consider is:

```
DP[i][j] = number of subsets with Bitwise
           OR j with elements 1 to j (index)
```

The recursive relations to compute the values are:

```
DP[i][((j-1)|arr[i-2])+1] =
          DP[i-1][ ((j-1) | arr[i-2]) + 1] + DP[i-1][j]
```

In this problem, we have considered a 2-dimensional array to solve this Dynamic Programming problem.

Key thoughts:

- If we consider a Graph problem and a Dynamic Programming approach for it, we may use an Adjacency Matrix.
- Any data structure where there is a clear relation between smaller structure and larger structure can be used in a Dynamic Programming point of view.

Conclusion

With this, we have come to the end of this wonderful book, but this is just a beginning in your deep understanding of Data Structures.

Algorithms are important and using the correct Data Structure transforms the approach completely.

Keep thinking about the different data structures and think of how you can upgrade the data structures like:

- If Binary Tree represents 2D space, how can we generalize it to N-dimensional space?
- If Hash Map can search in constant time, why in reality search is still a slow and challenging task?
- How a Binary Tree can help us accelerate searching? (Hint: Binary Search Tree)
- If Union Find has achieved near constant time performance, what is the performance if we include deletion operation?

Keep thinking and discovering.

Feel free to get in touch with us and enjoy learning and solving computational problems.